POEMS BY TOM CLARK

Easter Sunday

COFFEE HOUSE PRESS :: MINNEAPOLIS :: 1987

Earlier versions of some of these poems first appeared in the following books and anthologies: "Dispersion and Convergence" in AIRPLANES (1966); "And Now to the Stars," "Easter Sunday" and "The Elasticity of Solids" in THE SAND BURG (1966); "Alpha November Golf Sierra Tango" and "Climbing" in BIJOUS (1968); "Dark Continent," "The Daily News," "The Top of the World" and "Under the Flower" in STONES (1969); "The Sun" in THE WORLD ANTHOLOGY (1969); "Eos," "Back to the Front," "The Tire," "Disaster Site", "East Side Story", "Japanese Silk," "Gene Mirror," "Slow Lanes," "Air and Angels," "Vegetable Love," "The Byrds," "80°," "Hush, Hush" and "Ted Calling" in AIR (1970); "Duxbury Reef" in THE NO BOOK (1971); "Brainards" in GREEN (1971); "Gale," "Safari," "Casting," "Miles off the Farallons," and "At Bolinas Lagoon" in JOHN'S HEART (1972); "Poem Beginning with a Line by Smokey Robinson," "Story Line Without Plot" and "Various Small Fires" in SUITE (1974); "Ah—There," "Poetry Street," and "Water" in BLUE (1974); "Jan. 8," "One More Saturday Night," "And Don't Ever Forget It," "The X of the Unknown," "Radio," "Rounds," "March on the Mesa," "To Birds," "Stellar Launch" and "Infinity Electives" in AT MALIBU (1975); "Summertime" in 35 (1976); "Love," "Tarzan's Hand" and "Anomie" in WHEN THINGS GET TOUGH ON EASY STREET (1978); "The Shining," "Julia's Undergarments Viewed as a Vision of H2O," "To Leven Water," "Thoughts in Repression," "The Pie Maid," "Dover Beach" and "The Rebel Against Dogs" in THE MUTABILITIE OF THE ENGLISHE LYRICK (1978); "Love Poem That Requires No More Water Than Sagebrush" and "After Cézanne" in THE END OF THE LINE (1980). HEARTBREAK HOTEL (1981), THE BORDER (1985) and HIS SUPPOSITION (1986) were published as fine press limited editions.

The publishers wish to thank the National Endowment for the Arts for a Small Press Assistance Grant which aided in the publication of this book.

Coffee House Press books are available to bookstores through our primary distributor: Consortium Book Sales and Distribution, 213 East Fourth Street, Saint Paul, Minnesota 55101. Our books are also available through all major library distributors and jobbers, and through most small press distributors, including Bookpeople, Bookslinger, Inland, Pacific Pipeline, and Small Press Distribution. For personal orders, catalogs or other information, write to: Coffee House Press, Post Office Box 10870, Minneapolis, Minnesota 55458.

Library of Congress Cataloging in Publication Data

Clark, Tom, 1941–

Easter Sunday.
I. Title.

PS3553.L29E27   1987.   811'.54   87-27653
ISBN 0-918273-27-7 (pbk.:alk. paper)

Contents

Illumination

Easter Sunday

Someone has frozen the many-storeyed houses
Under this planetarium
A brilliant silence like a foghorn

A perfect frieze before the complications
Arrive with dialogue and
The olives of daily life

This brown Barcelona paper
Thrown onto the blue stone of the day
Makes everyone stop leaving

Through the light in a glass of wine you see them
Under the hot sky of the glacier
Placing their bets then boarding the funeral train

"Als Kind verliert sich eins im stilln . . . "

Sometimes children get lost in silence
under the hood of the big bell
we get lost where it is cold and dark
and the escaping bird
breaks its wing against the bell wall
the great rim cracks
a thread of light slips through
we are lost our breath
falters in silence a memorized note and
one day it sings of death
no longer guilty as the rain
we will come back
to the loved earth like flies clothed in snow

Dark Continent

The journey in darkness has a trivial jargon
For the cans of black coffee and ears like sprigs
Of an intelligent listening flower

This agitation is a kind of heavy wood
That you could hold a candle to
And never alter its unendurableness

There is nothing to do about voyaging
Fears except to jerk their brilliance
Out ahead of you like a rushlight like this

But what is illumined in the jungle large
Is a girl in narrow white sashes
Seated in your room at your writing desk

A Lamp

A lamp too near the floor
in the dim light thought   love   old letters
phone calls

turn to water
waves of matter like the cups and chairs
Memories

of places we will never return to and few
of us living in isolated apartments
will speak to each other again in the night

far apart and with our hands over our faces
asleep and looking at the ceiling
under a borrowed blanket

A Red Wild Flower in North Africa

The hand a halo
    does not touch it   it
  wavers

A red wild flower in North Africa
    shimmers

A stone in the wind   the sand
some dust blows in the sun   the wind
stops   we stand by the road
stops blowing   we stand by the road

A leaf blows against the stone

We are standing by the side of a road in the desert
some dust blows against a leaf
we look at it   all day

      the curious
    pelted foldedness
        its livery
      like a candy paper

a poppy?
the wind stops

Alpha November Golf Sierra Tango

From coast to coast
Voices of flight control
Are getting anxious

What is wrong suddenly
Is that I swallow a cold
Blast of air, I mean fright

Spill coffee on my book
And hear the kinks
In the great universe

The warp in the coffin
Phantom men fly out of
Anywhere in this world

Come in, come in, they call

Daily News

Dying day pinches the tot
He grabs my pen and beads
And plays into my hands
His father's skull glistens
Across his wife's white arms

The past bursts on a flower
And softly erases its bulb
We hear this going on all around
Night packs the traffic in cotton
And 1st Ave. fruit stands in opal

It is his first day to hurl a toy
But a gray torch rises in the future
Like a pair of scissors
The dark unravels towards
As I return to my newspaper

The Top of the World

Ignoring the longing of all fluid to boil and escape
Into a blue that is the memory of all movement
You rage jealously from the refrigerator
A zone where azure absorbs desire by becoming green
    and where
The logic of your gods loses out to the logic of an orange

And Now to the Stars

A kiss on the glove
At four blows
During lunch I dreamed of mud
But the neck of the waiter
A pink over the blue of the mud
Around your shoes
Was a something
A token I carried
To remember this love was like plastic

The Elasticity of Solids

You approach me carrying a book
The instructions you read carry me back beyond birth
To childhood and a courtyard bouncing a ball
The town is silent there is only one recreation
It's throwing the ball against the wall and waiting
To see if it returns
One day
The wall reverses
The ball bounces the other way
Across this barrier into the future
Where it begets occupations names
This is known as the human heart a muscle
A woman adopts it it enters her chest
She falls from a train
The woman rebounds 500 miles back to her childhood
The heart falls from her clothing you retrieve it
Turn it over in your hand the trademark
Gives the name of a noted maker of balls

Elastic flexible yes but this is awful
You say
Her body is limp not plastic
Your heart is missing from it
You replace your heart in your breast and go on your way

The Origin of Acrylics

The fishing on the swamp is fine
if slightly tragic
the big dark birds
fall out of the sky
and hit the turbid water
with a dead baby plop
like the words "dark green"

Disaster Site

A rara avis sails above the reactor disaster site
The track of the arrow through the feathers is televised
Chemical vectors are raking fire over and above
The smoke of the wreckage where the burning leaves
Release their brown numbers to the dry ice biplane
That ascends across now into later like tones
That detach themselves from the harmonic air ball
Of the planet as it screeches back into the past
Again and beyond into the future hyper-perfect

The Byrds

. . . a magic carpet ride

We are saturated by and
absorbed in the fluent
circuits of this energy

It snakes through you to be a
star in nova—all stored
force of the cosmos pours

Down the dorsal rosary
in phosphor flow, like
spinning discs in flicker—

Continuity, power, peace.
So in space ease seals me,
accepts me, I am released.

Dispensation

After Cézanne

When I went out to pick up the paper very early
I saw Y walking down the street with a large art book in
    his hands
There is a woman I know with poison honey in her bones
Who reveals truth to all of us by causing Y to suffer
Y drinks this poison honey you see
And later when his madness has faded
He begins to burn with a hard gemlike flame in pursuit of
    Cézanne

Stellar Launch

Not for nothing were you voted Miss Astronaut
Imploded past pleasure into knowing
Risking even injury because it's sweet pain
The huge space vehicle slowly turns
As it accelerates to lift off all silver
And take us to total flashing consciousness
With no ifs or thoughts of death or money
Simply 50 terrific synapses per minute caught
By starphoto lens each snowflake-intact
Each perfect each recorded *per eternitas* or at least
Until the reaper's wand hits the cranial noodleroni

To a Friend

She comes in colors
— Arthur Lee

Your body has an interesting
odor like flowers and your
skin has a very resilient
texture which I like to
compare with rubber balls

Once I saw you in a movie and
your hair looked black you moved
down a hillside like black fire
in a white dress the whole hillside
went up in blue smoke

And Don't Ever Forget It

Take off that apron
And put your red dress on
No
On second thought
Take off that red dress
And lay back
On my big brass bed
In your pink slip
The one with flowers sewn on it
Not the one
That certifies the registration of your auto

It's a lovely auto
I just don't like it
Because it has kudzu vines
Growing out of its body
And you know how I hate kudzu vines

Desert Star

O I want to say it was on Betelgeuse
Or Vega on a night blue like
This I first knew
How it felt
To be contacted by your hot Adriatic
No longer an island with its glass dice
Manhattan became your desert star
A man who caters ice
Sculptures to barbecues
Might know something about this
Obispo star shower sand geyser Pacific melt
You described the solar system to me by
Flexing the long ski
Run that slopes from your hip to your thigh

It's hard to recall those thermal signs
Lord Kelvin missed
When he defined all this for the first time
Beyond Concepcion toward Surf there are
Blue deuces being reduced to
Units only the cube knows
The way the coffee pushes itself
Into the sugar
Molecules the whole sense of the Gulf
Streaming into the floe
So that every time you look less
Of it's there
The night sky being invaded
By the color blue
Something about how you
Used to do this

Infinity Electives

I knew the tune
It was in my songs
Even before you came along
Yet only then did I perceive its meaning
This *you* I wished for

When I lifted its arms up
I noticed tiny wings
That's all I knew
The rest was Muselike
Anonymous this "you"

I guess those poems
Were like phonecalls to the future
I had your number
Knew what I was looking for
Even before I found it
In the face directory

Love Poem That Requires
No More Water Than Sagebrush

Moseying through the serious improbabilities of our time
Somewhere down that lonesome road that leads to total
    insanity
I make a left turn into the sparse sun
Of an autumn in which my sore foot takes over my entire
    identity
And forces me to bite the heads off innocent rattlesnakes
When what I really want to do is crawl up to the edge of
    your broken pedestal
And press my lips to the spot behind your kneecap where
    there is a tiny sac
That dispenses fragrant oils perceptible only to neurotics

Tarzan's Hand

I must complain the cards are ill-shuffled till
I have a good hand.
        —Jonathan Swift

"Believing something will happen
  Because I don't want it to
And that some other thing won't
  Because I do—" I wailed to the dealer—

"This is desperation." "Yeah?" he said. But then by
  Your graceful lines, your lioness' mane,
Your heat as you returned from
  Your day in the jungle, you relieved me from

What in myself was desperate,
  What even now insists on wishing
And believing. Still in the sheen of finely-breathing
  Blond hair that covers you,

By the flashing way you move from tree
  To tree, and from room to room,
Making it a bright full house,
  I find at least the light to see the cards I am dealt.

She

stays home
chained to loom program
nights days
till hair goes
gray like
old movies —
says "must go"
but stays due
to being
bound by
endless
duty to
weave fates
of future
humans —
too much
for one
non-contract
programmer

Eve

Never again will birdsong be the same
To do this to birds is why she came
This girl whose eyes are pale and mild
She puts the apple of the world on hold
Her hair is probably not real gold
Only a very good imitation of the Greeks'
Like a map of that world of early days
Where woman lives on a scarlet cloud
While man in colorless blunt noon
Splashes up at the blue variables
That pass by on an airplane of words
Into the sky which distributes gifts of
Rain and light over our lives equally
Infinite gifts we are unable to behold

Expansion

First Things

Waking
I experience in the void of my brain
the sensation of a thought
coming into being
first a soft ping
           then an explosion of sighs
that multiplies them centrifugally
like Miracle Grow
until they become a plenum

6:52 A.M.

Softly crushed
fog upon
the Flatirons

Time
to inspect for
grey hair

One Bird

Chanting
in a vast expanse
of concrete

To Birds

Sky full of blue nothing toward which you Magi
Move like dream people who are Walt Fraziers of the air
Sometimes the moves you make amaze me
For they will never happen again until the end of time

So shall I be like you   I don't think so   and yet to float
Above the rolling H$_2$O
On wings that express the mechanics of heaven
Like a beautiful golden monkey wrench

T'would be bueno

The Process

Two crows sew themselves onto the lace flag
Of that flying cloud whose cosmetic grace
Adorning the Plain Jane face of the day
Pins them in an unlikely halo of pale light
After one blast of which they dance away
Croaking shrilly as abandoned divas
Whose black scarves flap in the breeze
Over every home and panorama dark precise
Signs washed up on the air to be noticed
Out of a continuous process of succession

Aerial Math

The sky with its clumped
ranges of cloud motility
sloops out over the engine cowl
into a blue-decimaled expanse
of absolute light

Over San Pablo Dam

Proteus climbs
out dripping and scales
the soft rolling hills
a triathlete of beautiful green
earth buoyant
air full of cloud boilers
over dirty brown water

Duxbury Reef

Moonrise expresses spaces
in air, tides in the sea

illustrate old stresses
in nasal reef-voice, ah harmony
shimmering beyond choice
The silver surfer stands there, streaming

long hair laid out
across the night   so transposed.

Miles off the Farallons

That grey droning note
  I've heard every dusk

Neither owl nor foghorn
  but similar to both

The low fluted "day-is-done"
  of some unknown warbler

Atonally breathy memo
  of universal mysterioso

Tucks misty roses away
  in the dark's soft envelope

Safe under a lion's paw
  of starry numerology

Whose silver figures
  fleck the surf's Afro

Otherwise sparkling brassily
  into the liquid air

Jan. 8

Large yellow full moon
Sets over my shoulder
As I run home from Palo
Marin in pre-dawn cold

On my right the ocean shines
Like hot asphalt
Moment of inky mystery
And mirage

        Then in the east a Rose
Of Sharon saffron-ness sweeps
Over Mount Tam whose
Sleeping volumes are still
Snow-dusted

        And slowly
Overhead the whole bowl
Of sky brightens and expands
Counter-clockwise

At Bolinas Lagoon

Like a big tired buffalo
                    or ox
Mount Tam kneels beneath
                    a glittering ceiling
her blue and green
                    flanks rest, her shaggy
head settles
                    and drinks from the lagoon.
The fur of her underbelly is burnt and brown
cars wind down in it
                    like ticks. The top
of her head is yellow and balding
except where a few squiggly redwood tips
crest it. She rests, in the blazing
light of a June afternoon, as I do.

Life is not conditional. IF
is only a
          half-life.
A Whole Life—yours, mine, its—
can pass by in an instant. Hers
continues, like a music without notes,
unless you really strain
your ears to hear them, and maybe even then.

March 1st

Today there is new crocus white
and yellow yellow
aconite and a strange small
saffron flower held
back by ragged
flags of weed
the weed a carryover a dream
of August
all soft stooping
to the rain saturated

April 25th

Sweet taste of honey
in the warmth of morn

Cumulus flotillas
scud across the sun

Eucalyptus still in shade's
all black but at its zenith

There's this white lustre where
a westerly stirs it I guess

Lovely to be born
and live here to have seen it

Summertime

There's nothing left to do.
Air travels through the branches of alveoli
like a scuba diver with a vacuum cleaner
so that one deep breath fetches another from
in there where the breathing's stored
and after that a third and a fourth, fortunately.

80°

white butterfly

       dancing albino speck

          tiny hanky

    scarfs

       the swiss chard

there in the entero-system I imagine it cool

      Switzerland!

   pale sweet pea snows   wild radish lakes

    CABBAGE MOTH

on a day like this your thirst is easy to identify with

at five o'clock   eighty degrees of

wild July fire-and-jewel spectrum

humming bird   goat bell   bluejay feather etc.

Expansion

Distribution of moments.
Memory   Attention   Expectation.
A light plane, a feathery piano
solo. The time of everyone
in the world comes apart
in pieces, a slow quiet
dispersal. The poppies are still
furled into themselves
chilled morning maidens
but the musky red antique
geranium droops open as
do some purple blue
unnamables whose scroll
unrolls backward like Arabic.

The Days

one by one
and it's never done,
they show you their hearts, & then
they never speak again

they gulp for air the way a
thirsty animal gulps for water
they show you their hearts, & then
they never speak again

one by one
and it's never done,
but it radiates around
and it radiates around

Time Wash

The moment is a pearl-bearing shell
sealed at the bottom of the heart ocean
but tomorrow at the rising tide
shells will be cast up on the beach
as instants deposited by a water clock
all along the tonic scale of the sand
if not by the unheard undertow
which bails all eight rivers of the delta
and contributes to the formation of the reef

Transmission

Inside/Out

Jupiter symphony on phones over Iowa
35,000 feet above snow
cold air out there
a million cubic person-meters too many
emptied out to disperse into universe
in here
a lot of hot air
rushes toward stratosphere
a bright scatter
the notes in Mozart unfold
out the window slow
moving cloud parts some
kind of white fluff
feels aerated
warm light momentary
popcorn

Safari

Thoughts in
shorthand

head in
the clouds

that tone
goes on & on

when it ends
it's gone

"clear
as a

bell"

the ocean's
motion

the cat's meow

the phone rings
in the Sahara

the sky is blue
there is no one to talk to

March on the Mesa

The sandpapery candor of Bobby Dylan
Strikes a jejune note all of a sudden

Throw my ticket out the window
Throw my sneakers out there too

Mama said there'd be days like this
When rain pencils the sky

With an air of biological rigor
And visibility is grimly minimized

Tiny puffs of smoke speckle it
The harmonic spectrum is muffled

The tall white dog stands in the road
Shivering and shaking the water off

Water

The fog comes in flatter
than ever the air apparently

is blue somewhere not here
flat and linear the women

can't escape except through speech
so they go to the beach

when they've gone there
the air here's even heavier

because their light touch
stops holding it up

Back to the Front

A breeze blowing between the worlds
air here and the heavenly ones

Nearly knocks my head off
                on my front lawn

Where everything aspires to be sky
with delicate green arms

               That's what I want to do
go away on the light feet of my thoughts

            back Inside where nothing's palpable
As far away from here as possible

Casting

A tiny pressure of the wrist
against the fly rod and the real spins

the story thread runs out into
the night whose take-up reel's noiseless

lake's slickly alive with green
oily trout and eels moving like rubber

through the mind of Mother Nature
who croons to me on the bank

and passes her grassy fingers across
my eyes her delicate green arms

tangle lightly in my heart's ropes
I fall to the mat gasping

The Tire

The story thread runs out through your hands
To many places indicating them as snags
You take the tire apart   Even so the process
Solves its own knots as it continues gingerly
To slip out of your hands   There is always
A looseness open and moving it says here
In the event   Then why does every tug on the
Strings complicate everything ravelling
Up further the almost impossible ball   When
Know-how shows itself for what it is will Grace
Grow free and exact to award the useless
Virtues their place   Do I have to wrestle
With every thought on earth like this   I mean
Will an angel arrive and untangle them all

Zone

Light spray over a daisy chain of days
Did I drive right? Risky slopes
Deer start across hushed timber
Cool and the engine smoking guns
Dipping from third gear into second
I disappear into a thought shroud
Pushed by wind the ocean sends
Bears brush past dark eucalyptus
Whose underleaves turn silver where
The hawk dives in a flowing zone
That lights the road to the restless
Advance of trees and cars
A brown head whispers I'm
Your friend O lonesome
Man in the brunt of a huge wave

Gale

At forty unusual phenomena begin to occur. The
chimney
    whistles & the windows blister (rain).
At fifty to sixty it chases the cat in, breaks the
    pinebranch (Bishop), rips the eucalyptus leaf
    loose, wakes the baby, shakes the roof & bangs
    the door.
At seventy individual sounds subside in the general roar.
At eighty a flash heralds the arrival of Storm King
    in a black leather riding outfit (Coldwater Canyon,
    1941), accompanied by Mildred Pierce, stunning
    in a mauve chemise by de Kooning. Everybody's drunk
    flooded puddle in the bloody rain and driving
At this point transmission ended due to power failure.

Santana

The days wash away the days
The wind is a force
That drenches the heart

A dry heat that
Roars through the electric
Black oak forests
Where Sappho lays the table
With the burning ions of the pharaohs

In the Dark

It's not that no one's out there
but that nothing is
I feel like I'm talking to
the dust that blows
between the stars

Ted Calling

for Ted Berrigan

Waking up in the time zones
out of bed to the telephone
friendly transcontinental voice
and down the line by instant
across Pacific Mountain Central
to a tree-sized town's
frozen spaces where you are temporarily

warm in an office
behind Chesterfield green felt
blotter poems a prescription
bottle obitrol 10 milligrams
this year's home a department cell
in brick and glass Haven

Hall at two A.M.
your hot lava socks
propped on desk's manuscripts
a red mountain range those socks
major relief on the map
of that cold Midwest state
not New York thus a state of no
grace you light it up anyway

Hush, Hush

I know these radio waves
are being stored away
in my brain somewhere
even tho I'm not here
to pay any attention
    to them

They'll come back later as
frequency-modulated
variety shows and UHF cabaret

This is what I was thinking, Ted

For instance while I was
    writing this
the following music
    came into my head

Overture to *Sonata for Trumpets & Strings*
    by Henry Purcell
Miles Davis *Ssh . . . Peaceful*
Jimmy Reed *Hush, Hush*

Brainards

Joe's red poppies
on black
have presence

and when I look
at them I know
presence is energy

on a cool surface
a big hot process
inside steady eyes

Radio

Don't hurt the radio for
Against all
Solid testimony machines
Have feelings
Too

Brush past it lightly
With a fine regard
For allowing its molecules
To remain 100% intact

Machines can think like Wittgenstein
And the radio's a machine
Thinking softly to itself
Of the Midnight Flower
As her tawny parts unfold

In slow motion the boat
Rocks on the ocean
As her tawny parts unfold

The radio does something mental
To itself singingly
As her tawny parts unfold
Inside its wires
And steal away its heart

Two minutes after eleven
The color dream communicates itself
The ink falls on the paper as if magically
The scalp falls away
A pain is felt
Deep in the radio

I take out my larynx and put it on the blue chair
And do my dance for the radio
It's my dance in which I kneel in front of the radio
And while remaining motionless elsewise
Force my eyeballs to come as close together as possible
While uttering a horrible and foreign word
Which I cannot repeat to you without now removing my
     larynx
And placing it on the blue chair

The blue chair isn't here
So I can't do that trick at the present time

The radio is thinking a few licks of its own
Pianistic thoughts attuned to tomorrow's grammar
Beautiful spas of seltzery coition
Plucked notes like sandpaper attacked by Woody
     Woodpecker

The radio says Edwardian farmers from Minnesota march
     on the Mafia
Armed with millions of radioactive poker chips

The radio fears foul play
It turns impersonal
A piggy bank was smashed
A victim was found naked
Radio how can you tell me this
In such a chipper tone

Your structure of voices is a friend
The best kind
The kind one can turn on or off
Whenever one wants to
But that is wrong I know
For you *will intensely to continue*
And in a deeper way
You do

Hours go by
And I watch you
As you diligently apply
A series of audible frequencies
To tiny receptors
Located inside my cranium
Resulting in much pleasure for someone
Who looks like me
Although he is seated about two inches to my
 left
And the both of us
Are listening to your every word
With a weird misapprehension
It's the last of the tenth
And Harmon Killebrew is up
With a man aboard

He blasts a game-winning home run
The 559th of his career
But no one cares
Because the broadcast is studio-monitored for
 taping
To be replayed in 212 years

Heaven must be like this, radio
To not care about anything
Because it's all being taped for replay much later

Heaven must be like this
For as her tawny parts unfold
The small lights swim roseate
As if of sepals were the tarp made
As it is invisibly unrolled
And sundown gasps its old Ray Charles 45 of
 Georgia
Only through your voice

One More Saturday Night

Through the night
It snows on the
Sierras as it does
On the grave of
Apollinaire in the
Cemetery of Père
Lachaise
   and on
The radio I get
Truck music from
San Jose:
"Want to make it to
Amarillo by
Morning . . . "
   " . . . just
Because you ask me to."

The green oak
Burns weakly
In the grate
And as I write
In the window
Of the loft
The light
Turns blue

Friedrich & the Beyond

Considering the hyaline
liquidity
which in the extremely
deep spaces
of their backgrounds
are like swimming pools
filled up not with water
but with light
it could be said of Friedrich's canvases
that at first the lens
of the viewer
leans out on Infinity
while a second glance
opens the floodgates to Existence
which closes in all around
from the edges of the picture

When he worked
at painting a sky
no one was permitted
to enter his studio
because he believed
God was present

Alongside the Baltic
grey translucent light
fell on the lake of oil
that formed on the vertical
wall of the canvas
on the other side
there was nothing at all

Final Farewell

Great moment in *Blade Runner* where Roy
Batty is expiring, and talks about how everything
he's seen will die with him —
ships on fire off the shoulder of Orion
sea-beams glittering before the Tannhauser gates.

Memory is like molten gold
      burning its way through the skin
It stops there.
                      There is no transfer
Nothing I have seen
will be remembered
beyond me
That merciful cleaning
of the windows of creation
will be an excellent thing
my interests notwithstanding.

But then again I've never been
      near Orion, or the Tannhauser
gates,

I've only been here.

Rotation

Poetry Street

On Poverty Street, the disinterested
click of Dixie Cups on bakelite trays
reminds me that prose exists.

Animated Bedlam

If the wind sets off people's car alarms
is that legitimate inspiration
or merely nature's way of seeking social approval

Apocalyptic Talkshow

The man who calls up Larry King
at one o'clock in the morning
to recommend reading the Koran
as a cure for AIDS makes
more sense than the man
who calls up the KAL-X
Midnight Trax disc jockey
and says Fuck You in Korean
but then again the man
who just after the minor quake
calls in and says the tremor
let the air out of his basketball
sounds so much more like
the voice of the future

Avon Calling

Radio says Avon survey reveals American
women feel good
about themselves. Forty per
cent say they've never looked
better in their lives, eighty
per cent say they look
younger than their age, ninety
per cent say they're not afraid

their man will leave them
for a younger woman, but one
hundred per cent admit
they think they'll die
some day, and that's why
there'll always be an Avon.

Come In, Delphic Oracle

NPR pipes in KGNU
Broadcast of Harmonic Convergence
Dense with Messages of Impending Liftoff
Phoned in by correspondents from Stonehenge
To Macchu Picchu, Giza to Mt. Fuji
In accents from Jersey Low
To Ohio Broad. "I have very
Definite shivers going up and down
My spine at this time," says
The moderator, a latent Boulder
Sage. He's been beaming-up synchro-vibes
From the Sacred Sites. "Something
Is definitely happening. Why
Don't you stay on the line
As we go into our ritual now?" And then
Nine hundred networkers start humming
In unison like a traffic jam in the Holland
Tunnel. I can't help
Thinking first that if anybody out there
In the Van Allen Belt is really listening
This Galactic Signal from Earth will
Probably come as a shock relieved
By the knowledge they're out
Of our range; and second that I
Have only this to say to my fellow
Earthlings on this subject: I know
We are not feeling the same thing and
We are not feeling it at the same time.

Thought for the Nineties

now that the best and the
brightest only care about
being approved of as they
line up to watch *predator*

the time has come to admit
our future probably lies with
whatever green card applications
fawn hall didn't shred

An Event Left Out of the Chronology

Mr. Ghorbanifar took Ollie
North into the bathroom and told
a little story about predation.
"If the victim is not incapacitated
by the first blow, and the predator
must continue to engage him
in order to finish the kill,
there is a danger of sustaining
injury due to reprisal
by the victim," Mr. Ghorbanifar
said. "But certain species
have developed an efficient
solution to this dilemma.
The first was the sabre toothed
cat, with its marvelous
flanged jaw bone and
head depressing muscles
evolved to exert
a traumatic abdominal
bite." Ollie's eyes lit
up. "The second is
the great white shark
which like the sabre tooth
inflicts a single massive bite
to the underside of its victim
then retreats to avoid reprisal.
When the victim hemorrhages
or goes into shock, the predator
closes in to complete the kill."
Ollie smiled his little gap
toothed smile and said, "Neat idea."

Say What?

As a principle of government
in an entropic democracy
plausible deniability
is undeniably plausible

therefore absolutely correct
and almost as good as
the ability to say what
you remembered to forget

The Mechanics

For white people it's never too late to not learn something.
The Dr. Science bike class holds little poetry but
The mechanic in the back row's right who thinks
Toiling up hills takes its toll on old cranks.
In the gentle sloping wooded bowl a
Mile up Strawberry Canyon the Lawrence
Berkeley Lab building projects
Prepare the world for more new war
Toys. I've been told my late poetry's Savonarola
Reincarnated. And that makes sense.
The "slick easy poet" of Ted B.'s jokes
In *Train Ride* didn't survive the Future:
Now I spend my time whittling
Stakes to impale the present upon
Before I set fire to it, proving myself
A bore and a jerk. Still, what other
Reaction can poetry have? Sing
In lyric meter of these cool DOE-
and NSF-funded master-wizard mechanics
Climbing slowly up this sleepy pocket canyon
In their Toyotas to be destroyers
Of worlds like Death in the Vedas made
Modern and silly? I turn the bike's
Nose around and start the swift winding
Descent as a down-gearing Audi
Roars past me through the Security
Gate. Forget it, I tell
Myself: these guys aren't worth
Wasting a good stake on.

Behavioral Neuroscience

There are people who are paid
good money to stand around
in smock coats dosing rats
with drugs and pushing them
over to see which way they
fall while taking notes on
it. But can it be that *interacting*
in this *Administered World*
is as flat and bald as
that? Or as they used to
ask: What is Truth
anyway? Is it just Behavior?
Nothing is more easily
believed by us (said a
certain Viennese doctor) than what
without reference to the truth
comes to meet our wishful
illusions. Typology is odious.
We wish to feel more
complicated than (for example)
rodents. Yet what if there
are actually only two types
of humans left: those who do
the pushing, and those
whose special fate it is to
be numbered among the pushed?

Earth

a place where dogs race
around in circles
on dirt tracks
humans make them do it

once pleasant blue planet
now famous through
out solar system as set
of coordinates to avoid

Anomie

The color of stepped on gum
is the color of our time
the light of our time is
the light in the 14th St.
subway at 2 A.M. the air
of our time is the air of the
Greyhound depot Market
and Sixth it is prime time a passed
out sailor sits pitched
forward like a sack of laundry
in a plastic bucket seat
his forehead resting on
the movie of the week THE LONG GOODBYE

August, Mission Canyon

Stone bridge in Skofield Park
scene of FOR WHOM THE BELL TOLLS
get off prop Fuji on big rock
navigate babbling green arroyo
down to where white water tumbles
in small cascades over
very big white-ochre boulders
creating cool deep pools
where algae swim slip into water naked
except for large dirty foot bandage
just as Japanese touring party creeps
out of pittosporum Nikons popping

Rounds

When the Hound of the Basketball summons me
And blood passeth before my eyes
With a sort of scarlet thud
The Carson Show smiles of reality
Begin to fade
And I realize it's time to arise and go
To the school
To shoot a few hoops
In the saffron air of twilight

But when I drive in for a layup it's worth 50¢
In my imagination
Reminding me
Nothing is pure in this world
And that my agenda still includes
The acquisition of bank notes
Sufficient unto the purchase of goods
And transportation of same
The daily up and down of getting and spending
Living on a rubber band like that
Sometimes gives you the feeling you grew
The rubber tree yourself
The same tree from which came
This big red ball that yoyo's
Up and down
On an invisible string
Under your unemployed finger

The X of the Unknown

Sweet notes in dimensionless clusters
Eighth notes and fluttering cue balls
And Tibetan gongs in the side pockets
Those are what Charley Johnson heard
When he got his bell rung

He could stand but he could not see
He could hear but he could not talk
He could think but he could not walk
And over his head in the thought balloon
Little birds tweeted

So he continued to stand there
Until they came out and got him
And even then it was hard to lead him off
For he seemed like a man leaving his mind behind him
Somewhere there on the ground

Why I Can't Get Interested in Ron Darling

Though it remains a great pleasure to roll the names
and numbers around in what's left of
one's brain, that abandoned bowling alley lane down
which a compacted garbage ball of trivia always thunders
endlessly toward the rooted in concrete steel ninepins
of the facts of life and then bounces or slithers off into
the gutter uselessly, yet not without having diverted one
however briefly etc., still I'm having a harder and harder
    time every
spring connecting the nominative and statistical reality of
the players to these spoiled jockstrap boys from colleges with
a credit card between their teeth when they show up in
    florida
or arizona with a stockprofile in place of the old dizzy
    dean dream

Dreaming of Three Rivers

"I don't like the roads or the potholes,"
Phil Garner said, "but the people are great,
The people make the town . . . "
Snow fell gently on McKee's Rocks as he talked
Something we never see in the land of freeways
Where my next door neighbor's some guy I never met
And let's keep it that way.

"I too could grow to love the Iron City,"
I told Phil sincerely. "I could love the Ohio,
The Allegheny, even the dim Monongahela . . .
Especially if I had a big new house
In Fox Chapel, and played third for the Bucs—
Provided, that is, California would trade me at all."

Reggie at 37

To know the feeling
of being the one
nobody can replace
is temporary knowledge
. no matter how much
money you make a
day will come
when you can't buy a hit
and looking back
becomes a habit
there's always somebody
there behind you young
and waiting

Time Rotates but There Is Only One Season

The October light falls cold, and number 53
Steps across the infield toward his destiny.

The April light is sullen, and number 54
Walks to the mound once more. Now he knows the score.

Out beyond the stars the universe watches,
Counting beats of strange hearts between pitches.

Elevation

Love

Like ghosts,
   much talked about,
    seldom seen.

The Sun

after Desnos

I've dreamed so much of you
Walked so much
Talked so much made love to your shadow
So much that there's nothing left of you
What is left
Of me is a shadow
Among shadows but 100
Times more shadowy than the rest
A shadow that will come
To rest
In your life in which the sun
Is so much

Climbing

My heart in pieces like the bits
Of traffic lost in the blue
Rain confused I roar off into
To learn how to build a ladder
With air in my lungs again
To be with you in that region
Of speed and altitude where our bodies
Sail off to be kissed and changed
By light that behaves like a hand
Picking us up in one state and putting
Us down in a different one every time

Dispersion and Convergence

Like musical instruments
Abandoned in a field
The parts of your feelings

Are starting to know a quiet
The pure conversion of your
Life into art seems destined

Never to occur
You don't mind
You feel spiritual and alert

As the air must feel
Turning into sky aloft and blue
You feel like

You'll never feel like touching anything or anyone
Again
And then you do

East Side Story

It was the work of fortune
which brings joy and not pain only.
But can a winged thing become less?

I mean: in the divisiveness of love
two people pass through
the same instant separately

for all their awareness sighs
for life and not for each other
but in doing that it does.

Japanese Silk

Our arms sleep
Together under water

Air curves into the room
On feathers

Apple leaf light
Beneath the blankets

A butterfly of hair
In the breeze

Ah — There

the emerald mosque
   in motion
      every time a fern

touches
   the honey
      colored comb

she pulls
   through her
      fallen hair

Gene Mirror

The kaleidoscope
of evolution winks at me mysteriously from the
baby's face in ways that stomp on understanding

In the Lotus Pond

the lotuses come up and go pop
the small little bud in there is a complete
human being with all its parts intact
right down to happy laughing eyes
which snap and crackle with the truth
disguises having thus been rendered useless
in this paradise all you have to do
is lie back and go off like rice krispies

Under the Flower

After the sponge bath
Spice cake and coffee
In a sky blue china cup

Tiny clouds float by
Like bits of soap
In a bowl of very blue water

A happy baby sleeps
In a silky chamber
Under the trembling flower

Everything's safe there
Because nothing that breathes
Air is alone in the world

Slow Lanes

1

Cinematic blossoming of love gasoline

2

Blue windows behind the stars
    and silver flashes moving across them
  like spotlights at movie premieres

long cool windshield wiper bars

3

the butterfly gently opens itself like a fist
    dividing into wings   and drifting off
       over the cube's puzzled head

Air and Angels

The sweet peas pale diapers
Of pink and powder blue are flags
Of a water color republic
The soft bed turned back
Is a dish to bathe in them
This early in the morning
We are small birds sweetly lying
In it we have soft eyes
Too soft to separate the parts
Of flowers from the water
The angels from their garments

Vegetable Love

The green world thinks the sun
Into one flower, then outraces
It to the sea in sunken pipes.
But twisting in sleep to poetry
The blood pumps its flares out
Of earth and scatters them. And
They become, when they shine on
Beauty to honor her, a part of
Her laconic azure, her façade.

Eos

Solar emeralds melt and blend
In a slow flash flow
Silver eucalyptus sails above
Waves of lavender
We rise at daybreak
Light opens its pure brooch
Far out over the ocean
A machine of perfect touch

Poem Beginning with a Line
From Smokey Robinson

Got to be there so that she'll know
When she's with me she's home on
The air waves across the nation
Energy imagines it can move that way
But sleep hides her modes as nature's
Her skin is a dreaming surface
Blood drifts up through shadows
Light shifts on minimal rubies
The spots on water where fish breathe
Impossible to see them coldly
Or in some numerical epitome

Story Line without Plot

Her voice is heard and then the child's
Who is her daughter and they both sound
Very young they are both young girls
And they are talking in the garden
Under the pear trellis and their
Hair shines in the sun and the pear
Petals snow on them and they are one
Person going down through linear
Time but apart from it parallel
And talking and breathing again
And flashing and moving along that line

Various Small Fires

Warm ripe days   The sun floods the ridge with color
Before dawn slowly the reddish light implodes
And before dusk the moon floats up like a softball
Over the ocean   Starbright glimmers the weather
Satellite in a position akin to that of Venus
Or is it the skylab people coming down   Mutual
Interests unite people on earth and in the sky
Ah and the heart sighs to be so satisfied
It beats against the skin to bespeak love's beauty
The air brushes past it with a smoothness
Borne by zephyrs from somewhere like the Gulf Coast
Where the days are hard but the nights are long and warm
From various small fires static electricity causes
To crackle in the sheets and draw up our auras

Leaves

Leaves

These leaves
mind keeps taking
along watery
Piscean paths
down simple
sinks and seeps
and deep wet
weeping places
as course to
tidal seats where
sedge or marshy
reeds and grasses
express or currents
egress in pools

"flat round . . ."

flat round
nasturtium top
plate leaves with
gleaming pin
head size beads
of last night's
rain water still
balanced on
them

      pushed up
on long thin
green stems to
white morning

"small erect . . ."

small erect
green bougain-
villea leaves in
clusters move
unison as wind
lifts their stems

"mosaic veined . . ."

mosaic veined close
three point creeper
ivy leaves move on
vines over ground
leaf cover coming
to pavement break
off tiny furled buds

"redwood needles . . ."

redwood needles
blown down by
storm gather
under foot go-
ing slowly brown

"the thin trunks . . ."

the thin trunks
of trees with light
green mildew
covering them like
a skin just touched
by first rays winter
sun and slender
branches sway with
birds leaping
off them to
spring

Stare Up Into

halo chlorine
gas makes against
night's blackness

reeds grass I
had come this
far to part

tidal river
rushes through
wet silk cloth

moon beams
stacked up on
the runway

my thought a
mist of blood
around my heart

"scare tactic eternity . . ."

scare tactic eternity
soap white half moon
moves up through
winter sky's chill
steel blue

        cottony
mist hangs over
green lit water
wispy as ghost
trails of big
jet plane high
above

     in comes
another breath out
go saved
up thoughts like gas
leak in head pours
heavy ideas through a
crack in the world

"people . . ."

people
atrophy dream

tears leafy eddying
faraway buzz
planes above
  jets

Vegetable

sits on plate
stewed in own
juices wants
nothing knows
nothing just lets
fork slide in numb

Circling Back to "Leaves"

Stark empty armed plum tree traceries
this day Sunday morning the world *dank*
out there she said yet *warm* relatively
again after the forty cold days of the
world night December 16 to January 25 stuck
in torpor's bed of self and loss of creation

into which bed comes the one unaging
eternal thing she's rounded sweet beauty that yet
undoes and wakes and separates from all this worst
case torpor of self the one
best thing her own being like the world's large & with its
    color
warm and moist and coming green entry as the small
dark red plum buds still furled in
to themselves on long thin finger
branches start to swell out

The Mutabilitie
of the Englishe Lyrick

The Shining

Gism sat on Julia's skin,
   And shone too,
Like skin laden in
   Trembling dew;
It glittered to my sight
   Like a pure beam
Of reflected light
   On vaseline.

Robert Herrick 1591–1674

Julia's Under-garments Viewed as a Vision of H₂O

Whenas in flimsy things my Julia goes
    Swimming, then methinks how sweetly flows
The liquefaction of her clothes
    Like Neptune's daughter's.

Next, I cast my eyes and see
    How when she takes them off for me
They slip away hydraulically
    Like running waters.

Robert Herrick 1591–1674

To Leven Water

Pure stream, in whose transparent wave
My youthful limbs I wont to lave,
No torrents stain thy limpid course,
No rocks impede thy dimpling source.

Still on thy banks so gaily green
May numerous nerds and twits be seen,
And shepherds piping in the dales,
And lasses peeing in their pails.

Tobias George Smollett 1721–1771

Thoughts in Repression

It is as if, as toward the silent tomb we go,
We feel that we are greater than we know we know.

William Wordsworth 1770–1850

The Pie Maid

When the fit falls upon the morning rose
Or on the rainbow of the salt sand-wave
And thy mistress some rich recipe acquires
To glut thy sorrow with globèd peonies
And ruby grapes, and some rich anger shows,
Throw a bag over her head, and let her rave
And feed deep, deep upon her peerless pies.

John Keats 1795–1821

Dover Beach

The sea is calm to-night,
The tide is full, the moon lies fair
Upon the Straits; — on the French
Toast, the light
Syrup gleams but a moment,
And is gone
Down the hatch; for it is the light of France.
The cliffs of England stand
Made all of cardboard; a hand
Claps by itself. It gives itself a standing ovation.

Sophocles long ago
Heard it on the Aegean, and it brought
Into his mind
A state of crashing ignorance.

Matthew Arnold 1822–1888

The Rebel Against Dogs

Soaring through wider zones that pricked his scars
With memory of the old revolt from dogs,
He reached a middle height, and at the stars,
Which are the brain of heaven, he looked, and sank.
Around the ancient track marched, rank on rank,
The army of unalterable paws.

Algernon Charles Swinburne 1837–1909

Heartbreak Hotel

Stories Told by the Shores
of the Lakes of Africa

While the cash-green palm fronds sway, tears round as
coconuts tumble out of their eyes and roll down their
gleaming breasts, finally toppling over when they reach
the nipples, like big drops hitting the headlights of a
Porsche streaming down the Pacific Coast Highway in the
rain.

Character Is Fate

God was a woman. Mary was, frankly, God, John said. Yes, she was God; that was all there was to it. Falling in love with her had been like a religious conversion, John said. But you should not make a god out of another person. John was later to find this out the hard way.

Life Among the Canyons

Life among the canyons of Los Angeles. Explorers in jodhpurs and jungle hats drink gin slings on the porches of huts built on stilts. Cars pour up the freeway in the rain like homing salmon, ahead of the full lash of storm tilting in from the Pacific. Arriving home, we hear the women laugh. They run to fasten down the mats and hatches, of batting and bamboo, their skin-covered breasts flashing as the water streams down them. We will give them diamonds and record contracts and they will sit for paintings. Our portraits of them will end up in a museum whose architectural character is totally geometrical and unfriendly. The curator will be 19 years old and from the East.

Death, Revenge and the Profit Motive

Death is good, revenge is a waste of time, and who ever thought up the profit motive didn't understand either of those things, John said, tipping his head back to pour another drink into it. He was paying twelve hundred dollars a month to keep Mary in a glass and redwood shack with a hot tub in the hippest canyon in town, he said. And now she wouldn't even talk to him, and—he said—he was dying. "But only to get even!"

Heartbreak Hotel

Heartbreak Hotel is located among the abandoned oil derricks of Venice, California, on February 15, 1954. It is a small bungalow with a white picket fence. A man in a dirty undershirt stands in an open window staring at us. Suddenly a chill wind blows across the oily surface of the grey canal. We look up into the sky, which has no color at all. It frightens us and we turn to leave but as we begin to run, our first footsteps are drowned in the loud strains of "Heartbreak Hotel," which the man in the window is singing in the window of the Heartbreak Hotel.

The Border: A Play

The Border: A Play

The dark quiet ocean along the sandy shores of Veracruz,
where the exhausted Mediterranean flings itself on the
    beach
with a flash of scales, like a suicidal fish . . .

False hidalgos stripped to the waist conduct idle and
fractious dialogues under the moonlit palms, stopping
now and then to duel with knives; bodies flop to the
    sand . . .

Smoke partially obscures a vast bridge of timbers, from
beneath which a group of vagrants emerges to put on a
show for the rich — The Beggar's Opera . . .

A local pimp plays a highwayman in dirty scarlet coat
and muddied boots, daubing his lips now and then from an
opium cache kept in a wooden cigarette box . . .

Avarice and treachery, Gay seems to tell us in his play,
are not inbred but handed down from class to class
much as diseased legacies that infect history *in*
    perpetuum . . .

Brandy-swilling junior officers like characters out of
an Edwardian farce step forward to meet the sleazy,
bullet-headed opportunists who are leading the
    uprising . . .

Watching, we are sensitive to the smallest eddies and
currents of emotion, the equivocations of the sickly helots,
the muddy threats of the lords of gibbet and blade . . .

The songs intermingled with the drama create disjunct
time shifts that completely obscure the sense of the
text, a confusion increased by the appearance of the
    musicians   131

They are a band of sawed-off natives armed with clarinet,
guitar, concertina and violins, instruments they wield
    more like
weapons, bickering even as they play, and sometimes
    attacking the audience . . .

There is a hazy neon image blinking on and off above the
stage: "Frontier . . . Frontier . . . Frontier," beyond
    which we just
make out the vague, dissolving image of a suspension
    bridge . . .

Its elegant span arches into an unknown of
which we can perceive only slight hints, like the wind
that whistles constantly in the brown-gray obscurity . . .

Off to the left a new group of musicians approaches
Cautiously, midget-ruffians in severe dark suits, toting
    instrument-cases,
clutching the guardrails, chattering among themselves . . .

Shrill and inexplicable noises occasionally rise
from the empty eyesockets of these dilapidated mummies
who, we discover, are only "pretending" to be musicians . . .

Actually they are demented rag dolls without brains
whose schizophrenic jerking movements, we understand,
are controlled from somewhere offstage . . .

The absent *metteur-en-scene* is, we sense, also a diabolical
menteur-en-scene who wishes only to deceive
us with enigmas and illusions of manipulated space . . .

The lighting effects are mechanically conceived attempts
to make us uneasy, to split our personalities
and confuse us, in which they are completely
    successful . . .

Wind and fog machines, revved up full blast,
make the single gas footlight at the front of the stage
seem inexpressibly hopeless since it illuminates
        nothing . . .

But now an Indian summer glow begins to descend from
the false ceiling, creating an amazing likeness of the
valley of the St. Lawrence in October . . .

Six thousand men in 350 boats, forming a procession
five miles long, slide down the great river from
the left of the stage toward the right . . .

As the flotilla approaches center stage we gradually
realize that the captain is either drunk or badly reduced by
opium: he teeters precariously from the bow of the
        primary boat . . .

The men of the riverborne party are groaning terribly and
        clutching
their bellies, warning the audience to stand back: they are
suffering from a virulent form of amoebic dysentery . . .

From behind large clumps of bushes at stage right, the
        boats are fired
on by war parties of Indian stragglers, old hoboes
and red-satin vamps in Dracula sweatshirts . . .

The flotilla slows and twists agonizingly around
every channel as the river takes a new and more
complicated, intricate shape with winter coming on . . .

There is a sense of desolation, an Arctic chill
in the air and an unnerving desperation about the
landscape that tells us: we are crossing the border . . .

His Supposition

For Heiner Müller
whose supposition this was

His Supposition

His supposition is he's moving on foot through woods
The breeze is hot it grips like slow paralysis
Its source and direction are not apparent
The leaves undulate like serpents

Static halflight of a strange protracted dusk
Through which he moves keeping his eyes down
Trying to pick out the exsanguinated
Carmine trail   The earth keeps wavering

He keeps tracking a beast Fate
Sent him out to deal with capture battle
In the difficult halflight nights and days
Are hard to tell apart   The fact that

The earth seems to wobble when his feet
Fall on it and also to inhale
And exhale   Remains a mystery
As also the question of the solidity

Of the epidermal earth layer imposed
Over depths as yet ungauged
And liable at any moment to give way
Dispatch him flailing to the earth's ulterior

So he picks out his steps with caution
Causing the earth which had previously collapsed
Downwards under his boots to now begin
To rise up toward them as if sucked

Or so it seems   And the weight of his feet
Seems to increase proportionately
Either because of the earth's pulling down at them
Or because the farther he walks the heavier they get

Or because of something else   These spinning breezes
That play through the woods like dust devils
Boiling up out of the ground
Producing visions that make him dizzy

Indicating to him that his feet are neither
Increasing in weight nor being tugged down
By the earth but that the pumping velocity
Of his blood is slowly dropping

And this comes as a consolation relaxing him
And giving him the strength to move with greater speed
Or perhaps only the illusion of speed
Since the increasing contact of his body with branches

May equally be due to the increasing
Centrifugal velocity of the spinning breezes
More and more branches brush against his skin
At first a gentle sidelong contact

Barely noticeable on his epidermis
Later becomes increasingly insistent
Leafy feelers reaching to encircle
His limbs as if measuring him for a suit

The suddenly quite dense woods closing in
On all sides concealed eyes the trees regard
Him with an interest that is almost personal
Or really isn't it that some hidden

Agency is waiting behind the trees
Maneuvering these circular breezes
Frisking him going through his pockets turning
Him inside out more or less undressing him

Exposing him and in this way giving rise
In him to the surmise that this is perhaps
No longer a "woods" at all that name having
Survived from an earlier description

Which has become completely anachronistic
And leaping from that thought it next occurs
To him that if this woods is no longer
A woods but instead a complex intentional system

Of whose name he has not yet been informed
Then indeed it may also be that the monster
Toward which he supposes he is moving
Has equally and with the same horrible ease

By which it once turned Time into
Shit discharged in space   Turned itself too
Into something one can't pin down
With the oldfashioned appellations "beast" or "monster"

And for that matter the nomination systems having
    obviously changed
This "he" who has no name can't be completely
Certain that which speeds or crawls
Over this contracting expanding earth is actually itself at all

Looking down at his legs to resolve this sudden doubt
He is abruptly clutched much tighter
By the woods as though a screw's been turned light
Swift pincers now enter his anatomy examining

Its interior arrangements   The pain is intense
A huge yell wants to issue from his mouth
But he overcomes it   Starts to run   A furious
Standstill   No headway   The grip of the woods

Gets tighter   Tighter   The harder
His legs pump the greater pressure
He feels internally as the clutching woods
Squeeze his bones against his viscera

And the anxiety of this suddenly implodes
Into knowledge   It is the woods
Itself that is the monster he is pursuing
And it carries his legs along

Breathing through these swirling breezes
And gasping in these shakings
Of the earth   And the exsanguinated
Trail he dogs is nothing but

The life fluid of his own body
Drained continuously by the monster
Out of curiosity to see how much
Of it there is   And then a flash

Illuminates the woods and he sees
An x-ray of the inside of his own
Body in the form of a circuit diagram
Showing all the movements of nerves and blood

And then he hears the noise
Of his own voice in laughter taking
Over from himself to stifle
His endless complaints   It comes

As a change for the better
Because now he knows   the conflict has begun
Run   foresee   attack   outflank   evade   maneuver
Put things in a different order if you can

Evade by manuevering   Attack
By outflanking   Run by attacking   Foresee
By evading   Play the whole tape
Backwards   Inside out   Rearrange the parts

Change the sequence   Practice the waiting
Action of the assassin and
The aggressive action of the executioner
And the defensive action

Of the victim and then shuffle
The order of the roles and run
Through the whole thing again very
Slowly with maximum attention

To the position of digits   Motion of arms
The peripheral sweep of vision
The work of nerves   The fingernails   Elbows
The muscles twitching on call   The trees

Clutching pulling from all sides
They crush his skeleton up against
His teeth in a chokehold recalling
Something lost   The experience of birth

The trees become a sudden screen in front of him
The disturbing program the unfolding
Experience scene the replaying back
To the beginning before this struggle began

The memory is dental   The teeth
Splitting   The blood rushing out   The
Cartilage tearing open   Big holes
Appearing in the skin   The memory

Of the original struggle becomes
The present struggle   The insinuation
Of long whiplike fingers lined with
Sucking claws causes a discomfort

Which is impossible to separate
From the unpleasant sensations of
Blades moving in circles and ripping
In or pounding   Propelled by large weights

Which in turn are impossible or very difficult
To separate from the fragmented slow
Detonations sucking explosive floors
Optic daggers cultures of fatal slime

Themselves very difficult to separate from
His own mouth legs eyes arms
Through which he is able to register
The pain and through the pain

He is able to understand the overpowering
Superpain which extends inward
Toward the center of the experiencing
Being destroying emotionality for all time

By a process of deconstruction
That occurs over and over   Breaking
Him down into smaller and smaller
Pieces which he continuously rebuilds

Like someone reconstituting an ancient city
From a pile of shattered fragments with
The aid of what may be a completely
Inaccurate map   So that the skeleton

Of himself which he puts
Together in this way comes out
All screwy   Knees in the middle of
Arms   Elbows every which way

Toes where there should be fingers
Hip bone floating on one
Shoulder   Tab A Slot B   Field
Surgery   Performed with No Time

To consider what he is doing
And scattered harried by noises sounds
In his head songs in unison
Crooning Don't do it this way

You've got it all wrong It's
Useless Forget it Quit trying
These faulty rebuildings
Are performed under the trying conditions

Of having to construct some effective
Weapons of defense on what's really
An emergency basis as the
Weird forest crushes in   He needs

Tools to twist bend restrain
The sucking claws talons crushing
Pincers and fluid draining nozzles
Of everday life   To delay this

Rebuilding he stalls in hopes of absolute
Disintegration a last minute
Deus ex machina conquest by nothingness
Bringing about a final and total

Defeat translated victory which would amount
To the death of the monster although
Of course the void waiting to rush in
May itself be the secret adversary

In this struggle since it is always
Out there with his name and number
On its list   The pale blank lack
Of sound now surrounding him like cotton

Stuffing indicates the end of the struggle
Is closing in as night on a road
Along which he begins to glimpse illegible
Signboards of altering motive projected

Up by this mechanical
Monster known formerly as himself
But now changing every few
Breaths footsteps movements

And he sees that each time his
Mind moves it is altered
Again by his trials expirations
Thoughts becoming its signature.

Songs of Creation

The Song of the Drowned Ghost in the Pool

The song of the drowned ghost in the pool's
heard like an admission that the soul's
three thousand years bereft in us, as a slow

settling like snowflakes in a paperweight
somebody dropped that long a time ago
of these crystals through the gene,

pearly drifts of the first stuff which drove
space craft out to range across gates and
reaches of solar systems, seeds and puffballs

of eternity. The song drifts and echoes down
through the still translucent glass-
like water, as a helmsman compels the planet's never-

stopping forward path toward the outer
lights that glint and twinkle like some far Las
Vegas seen across the desert at night on flashing

pari-mutuel boards of creation.

"The blue planet lights . . ."

The blue planet lights
up and quivers with the strong
sap surge under hoof-toe drum beat
of that elfin guy who as
he plants his soft tongue like a hymn
upon her 80 million photo
electric cells also gives voice
to the echoic chorus of love that climbs
up to the solar plasm which pulses
across the magnetic amphitheatre of the cosmos

And everything is everything and
everything answers everything
the sky receives the birds and the plains
and the forest accept the
mammals the oceans accept the fish and
everything's enclosed in one
big ring of space feeling
and even humans are included in God

The sun shoots high out over
the Pacific to the west and when
it goes down into the cold water
at night it lights up the under
sides of the cirro cumulus clouds
with bands of pink that go
over into gold and rosy yellow
against the great deepening blue

And then the stars spring up shining
like sand grains on a beach at night
and are driven across the whole body
of the sky like worlds that voyage
across the black horror of space
all night just to hear her single tone
that's distilled out of the ether a
single note that becomes shaped
into an embryo in the huge crucible of life
so once more some new kind
of monkey may come again and settle
in the trees above rivers that
murmur with mysteries all night long

The Electrical Storm of Heraklitus

"The blue planet lights up" mid-afternoon
lightning tears open the
dark sky and in its gleam lights
up and lets all individual
things be seen in clear outline
outside Doe Library under ten-storey-high
campanile students stand gaping holding
their books staring
skyward over campus roofs and trees to where
lightning streaks across the whole horizon to the west
Zeus stamping pounds out his wild beat "Lightning
steers the whole universe" says
Heraklitus Fragment 64 *ta*
de panta oiakizei
keraunos meaning the whole created
kosmos the "all things" Zeus
steers through their "coming
into being" Fragment 1 *ginomenon*
gar panton the plural
universe is altered the single
bolt out-breaks flashing forth and crashes
to earth at the summoning
of Zeus the Helmsman who in this great act of sudden
determinate stamping changes
earth's genetic stock forever
imprinting his will upon all creation
I ride home from the library in the rain myself carrying
like my books this imprint of Time

The Blue Dress

I close my eyes
and see you at the age of 30
beyond the mist of affect
in your blue dress
so slim and viennese
in the sharons' picture gallery
at tissa's party
on a stormy night in 1974
with the ocean roaring
against the breakwater
I find you there with
all my projections
withdrawn at last
and what appears is
you in your blue dress
in the real objective secret
of your self
and the total beauty of your self
in your blue dress
which comes from forgotten existence
thickets of the 19th century
whose density disappears in
the evaporation of this thought
but nature never dies in time
because it never really existed
outside this recurrent bewildering
intensified mind ignition garden
we call creation